Consciousness Archaeology

Maximus Freeman

BALBOA.
PRESS

A DIVISION OF HAY HOUSE

Balboa Press books may be ordered through booksellers or by contacting:

Balboa Press
A Division of Hay House
1663 Liberty Drive
Bloomington, IN 47403
www.balboapress.com
1 (877) 407-4847

Because of the dynamic nature of the Internet, any web addresses or
links contained in this book may have changed since publication and
may no longer be valid. The views expressed in this work are solely those
of the author and do not necessarily reflect the views of the publisher,
and the publisher hereby disclaims any responsibility for them.

The author of this book does not dispense medical advice or prescribe
the use of any technique as a form of treatment for physical, emotional,
or medical problems without the advice of a physician, either directly
or indirectly. The intent of the author is only to offer information
of a general nature to help you in your quest for emotional and
spiritual well-being. In the event you use any of the information in
this book for yourself, which is your constitutional right, the author
and the publisher assume no responsibility for your actions.

Any people depicted in stock imagery provided by Thinkstock are
models, and such images are being used for illustrative purposes only.
Certain stock imagery © Thinkstock.

Printed in the United States of America.

ISBN: 978-1-5043-2529-5 (sc)
ISBN: 978-1-5043-2530-1 (e)

Library of Congress Control Number: 2014922271

Balboa Press rev. date: 02/04/2015

I dedicate this book to the following four authors whose books were indispensable in my preparation and completion of this book: Dr. David R. Hawkins, Dr. Robert Holden, Gary Zukav and Linda Francis.

Contents

Caveat Emptor

There is only one thing that I absolutely know for certain and that is that I know absolutely nothing for certain. Everything that you are about to read is nothing more than speculation -- nothing more than my current view of what calibrates as true to me in this present moment. As I continue to evolve, so will my views...

Foreword

During the artistic creation of this book, the following original terms and definitions intuitively arose within my conscious awareness:

Belieflessness: A very deep sense of knowing nothing for certain; going with the flow and practicing a complete absence of resistance to what is; being mystically stricken with the inability to form an opinion or judgment about anything; surrendering or letting go of all preconceived notions and conditioned thoughts; humility.

Consciousness Archaeology: The deep and mystical exploration of our conscious and unconscious minds with the intention of uncovering the core of our being and lifetimes of previously unexamined experiences.

True Worth: Our natural state of pure innocence; a condition of perfection and completeness.

Uncovery: The unveiling mechanism for dissolving the obstacles that are obscuring our true worth; the unlearning of conditioned thoughts and preconceived notions.

Like the sun behind the clouds, our true worth is always there; it just needs to be uncovered.

Prelude

Over the past 19 years, the books that have been most helpful to me are the ones that leave me with useful strategies long after I have finished reading. Many books are informative and helpful, but usually within a week or two, I have forgotten most of what I have read and have resorted back to my old comfortable ways of being. However, when a book provides simple, practical mechanisms that I can use on a daily basis, I never forget the valuable lessons learned and I continue practicing and benefiting from them every day. Therefore, it is my intention to introduce a variety of mechanisms that I hope will be just as beneficial. The purposeful repetition of many of the mechanisms throughout this book may seem redundant, but my experiences have proven that lessons are often best learned through repetition.

My favorite mechanism is The Letting Go Mechanism from the book *Letting Go: The Pathway of Surrender* by Dr. David R. Hawkins (764,774). Essentially, letting go is a mechanism of emotional non-resistance. Instead of resisting our emotions through suppression and repression, letting go allows them to naturally run their course.

According to Hawkins, "Suppression and repression are the most common ways in which we push feelings down and put them aside" (649). These defense mechanisms eventually lead to compression, which is exhibited as anxiety, stress and irritability. Letting go, on the other hand, leads to decompression.

Hawkins explains The Letting Go Mechanism as follows:

> Letting go involves being aware of a feeling, letting it come up, staying with it, and letting it run its course without wanting to make it different or doing anything about it. When letting go, ignore all thoughts. Focus on the feeling itself, not the thoughts. Have the feeling without resisting it, venting it, labeling it, fearing it, condemning it or moralizing about it. A feeling that is not resisted will disappear as the energy behind it dissipates (764,774).

Just because an emotion disappears doesn't mean we won't experience it again. In most cases, our stubborn feelings and emotions resurface regularly. Each time they reappear, we must let them go. Eventually, the energy behind them will lessen and we will feel relief. The Letting Go Mechanism isn't always a quick fix; it is more of an ongoing, life-long practice of non-resistance.

Letting go starts with self-honesty. We cannot let go of something that we don't fully understand or are unable or unwilling to even admit exists. Hawkins offers this valuable insight:

> We [all] carry around with us a huge reservoir of accumulated negative feelings, attitudes and beliefs. The accumulated pressure makes

us miserable and is the basis of many of our illnesses and problems. We are resigned to it and explain it away as the 'human condition.' We seek to escape it in myriad ways. The average human life is spent trying to avoid and run from the inner turmoil of fear and the threat of misery. Everyone's self-esteem is constantly threatened both from within and without. If we take a look at human life, we see that it is essentially one long elaborate struggle to escape our inner fears (621).

My self-honesty started when I fully accepted that I was just like everybody else and I also carried around a huge reservoir of accumulated negative emotions. This acknowledgment enabled me to whole-heartedly begin the practice of letting go.

Book One

The Uncovery of Our True Worth

*Breathe in and slowly absorb
and embody the transmissions
to follow...Namaste*

Introduction

We are Spiritual-physical beings, eternal Spirits temporarily residing in physical bodies. It is the Spirit's intention to use the body in this lifetime of earth experiences to evolve and mature. When the body passes away, the Spirit moves on. In this book, I will refer to the body as the person or self and the Spirit as the Soul.

Each person begins his or her earth-life experience in the state of pure innocence and belieflessness. In this state we have a very deep sense of knowing nothing for certain and have no preconceived notions or conditioned thoughts. We simply go with the flow and do not resist anything. Low self-worth does not exist, and ideas of good and bad or right and wrong are incomprehensible. This condition of perfection and completeness is our true worth.

However, slowly but surely, through nurture and nature, we are programmed with beliefs, opinions and conditioned thoughts. From these we create a picture in our mind of what the ideal person should look and act like. When we cannot possibly live up to this unattainable standard, our insecurities are born and our self-worth plummets.

Eventually, the discomfort of feeling unworthy becomes unbearable and some of us reach out for help. And in this moment, many of us see for the first time that there is a choice; we don't have to feel miserable. There are steps we can take that will bring us back to our natural state of belieflessness and true worth, and the first step is to uncover the roots of our insecurities.

For the last several years, every time I felt insecure, I desperately sought the reason why, and it always came back to my low self-worth. When initially searching for answers, I typed the following into Google: "Is low self-worth really at the core or root of all insecurities?" The very first item that appeared was this quote by Gary Zukav: "Lack of self-worth is the fundamental source of all emotional pain. A feeling of insecurity, unworthiness and lack of value is the core experience of powerlessness." Once our self-worth is compromised, shame is usually the consequence. What exactly is shame? According to Sandy and Michael Graham, on their website www.shameresilience.com, "Shame is the feeling we experience when we believe ourselves to be inadequate in some way. A more painful experience of shame is the sense that we are so flawed that we don't deserve to be loved or to belong."

Therefore, shame could be viewed as the root of most of our insecurities. Now that it appears that we have found the primary root, how do we remove it? By developing a better understanding of some of the negative attributes that exacerbate shame.

The Perfect Judge

Perfectionism: Striving for flawlessness and setting excessively high performance standards accompanied by overly critical self-evaluations and concerns regarding others' evaluations.

Judgmentalism: Making judgments about the conduct or attributes of ourselves and others; a judgment of the rightness or wrongness of something or someone.

Perfectionism and judgmentalism seem to go hand-in-hand. I've noticed that whenever I judge myself as being unworthy, perfectionism is usually the trigger. The behavior pattern begins every time I experience feelings of inadequacy, and in an effort to prove my worthiness, I overcompensate by trying to be perfect. When I fail to reach that unrealistic and unattainable standard, I once again feel unworthy. What a vicious cycle!

Furthermore, I often hold others to these same standards and think less of them when they fail to achieve these goals. This belittling or degrading of others triggers my feelings of superiority or false pride, and momentarily and artificially boosts my sense of self- worth. Conversely, it is only a matter of time before I encounter a person who is smarter, taller, richer, more attractive or better liked. When this occurs, he or she will inevitably knock the chip of superiority off my shoulder and propel my cascade back down into the low self-worth trap of inferiority and shame.

I asked myself how I could put a stop to this see-saw of conflicting emotions, and while exploring other factors that may be motivating these judgmental behavior patterns, I stumbled upon Carl Jung's theory of mirroring. He said, "Everything that irritates us about others can lead us to an understanding of ourselves." As hard as it may seem to believe, it is quite possible that the irritating traits we see in others are reflections of ourselves.

When I am with people who whine and complain, seem oblivious of their own shortcomings, make know-it-all declarations and are unavailable or disagreeable, I find that this triggers my irritability, anger and eventual condemnation.

Is Jung right? Does this disdain of others really mirror back to me that I whine and complain, am oblivious of my own shortcomings, make know-it-all declarations and am unavailable and disagreeable? Holy crap! Perhaps it does. No wonder I cringe and then judge others when they exhibit these traits. They are essentially holding up a sign in front of me with a list of all my shortcomings. What a frightening and eye-opening revelation!

Now that we have a better idea of why we may act the way we do, how do we move away from this negativity? By allowing our Inner-Teacher to guide us!

Inner-Teacher

Our Inner-Teacher is our Spiritual guide. This Divine essence continually sends the Soul guidance in the form of emotions and intuitions, and by listening for this guidance we no longer have to search for answers outside of ourselves.

The first step in becoming receptive to this guidance is to take notice of all our emotions, as they are messages from our Inner-Teacher. This emotional guidance system is constantly running in the background and signaling the Soul when there are suppressed or repressed emotions that we need to address. Once we start to notice these emotions as they arise, we begin to better understand what it means to be the witness or observer of our emotions instead of the participator or knee-jerk reactor.

Gary Zukav's detachment mechanism "On the Bridge" offers a helpful strategy for noticing the presence of these emotions and simultaneously becoming the witness-observer. In the book *The Heart of the Soul: Emotional Awareness,* he suggests that we utilize the following practice whenever we feel any painful emotion, such as anger, jealousy, sadness, depression, vengefulness or greed:

> Imagine that you are in a river of these emotions.
> Now imagine yourself getting out of the water
> and walking out onto a bridge. You look down

> at the river and watch it rushing below you. The
> water in the river represents your emotions. Let
> this water flow below you while you watch. At
> the same time, feel the river of energy flowing
> through your body. Allow yourself to feel these
> emotions with detachment, like watching the
> river flow below you while you are on the
> bridge (108).

Noticing, witnessing and observing are all forms of mindfulness, the maintaining of a moment-by-moment awareness of our thoughts, feelings, bodily sensations, and surrounding environment. By practicing mindfulness, we become much more aware of our response patterns and gradually learn how to make the shift from the experiencer or victim of our emotions to the unattached witness-observer.

The experiencer or victim often displays impulsive reactions to uncomfortable stimuli. Through mindfulness, the witness-observer discovers the benefits of pausation. This hesitation is a display of patience. By calmly enduring instead of reacting, we give ourselves the opportunity to appropriately respond, and this often keeps us out of trouble.

Our Inner-Teacher also sends the Soul positive messages in the form of intuitions. For my entire adult life I can remember receiving intuitive messages. My first recollections were 20 years ago, oftentimes when I was in the shower. This was a place where the rushing of the water drowned out all other noise and distractions. This quietude created the perfect receptive atmosphere for intuition. I still remember charging out of the shower, naked, and running to my bedroom to quickly jot down my thoughts before I would forget. I also kept a pad and pen near my bed for the many times I awoke with my head full of thoughts I didn't want to lose.

As time went by, these intuitions began to occur more frequently and much more powerfully. I remember a five-year span when I would often wake up in the middle of the night in a panic, with an unsettling feeling that somebody or something was trying to get my attention. These episodes left me with a strong sense that there was something monumental brewing behind the scenes. It wasn't until more recently that I finally discovered what that was.

The epiphany started with a visit to Barnes and Noble where I went to peruse the self-improvement and spirituality sections. I slowly worked my way through the alphabet of authors and occasionally pulled out a book or two that caught my eye. But as soon as I got to the H's, I knew that I had found exactly what I had been directed to discover. The second I touched *Power vs. Force* by Dr. David R. Hawkins, I sensed that something magical had just happened.

Reading this book gave me an entirely new perspective on life. Hawkins' simple, yet practical messages helped me to see the non-linear side of the Universe for the first time. Up until that day, I was living the life of a five-sensory being; thereafter, I was clearly on a multi-dimensional, limitless journey.

Before this partial awakening, I seemed to receive intuitive messages only involuntarily. However, as my awareness grew, I learned that I could summon intuition on my own.

I often do this by asking my Inner-Teacher questions such as: What exactly am I feeling? Why do I feel this way? and How should I proceed from here? I use this strategy most often when I take my daily walk in the woods, and usually, by the end of the walk I have answers to all my questions. I can do this exercise anywhere at any time and the results are always extraordinary. The key to its success is shutting down the thinking mind, listening for guidance and paying attention to what arises.

For most of my younger years I relied primarily on external teachers and gurus for guidance, and several of these teachers seemed to say the same thing: There comes a time to throw away all of the books, teachers, audios, videos and retreats and just be, and have faith that all future guidance shall come from within and that guidance shall come from your Inner-Teacher.

The first significant intuitive message that I received from my Inner-Teacher was crucial to all of my future growth: it was finally time to forgive myself.

Self-Forgiveness

In Robert Holden's *Happiness Now!: Timeless Wisdom for Feeling good FAST,* he says, "Through self-forgiveness, you wipe away your fears, you undo your doubts and you wash away all darkness to reveal the Light of your unconditioned Self (true self). Forgiveness gives you back your freedom" (85).

The following is my self-forgiveness meditation that was inspired by Robert Holden:

> *I forgive myself for all of the times that I have criticized and condemned myself.*
>
> *Through forgiveness, I am reminded to honor and respect myself.*
>
> *I forgive myself for thinking that I am bad.*
>
> *Through forgiveness, I am reminded of my goodness.*
>
> *I forgive myself for thinking that I am unworthy.*
>
> *Through forgiveness, I am reminded of my worthiness.*

I forgive myself for being judgmental.

I forgive myself for being scared.

I forgive myself for making mistakes.

Through forgiveness, I am reminded that I am human; and like all humans, I have inherent limitations and shall occasionally make inappropriate choices.

Through forgiveness, I am now able to be compassionate with myself.

Through forgiveness, I am now able to accept myself.

Through forgiveness, I am finally able to love myself.

The first time I practiced this meditation, I sensed that something profound was happening. Each line I read had a dramatic effect. Negativity was abating, the burdens of guilt and remorse were lifting, and for the first time in my life, I felt as though I was finally starting to forgive myself.

My self-inflicted grudges and harsh criticisms were beginning to dissolve, and the further I read, the more intense the joyful sensations became. Toward the end, tears of happiness and relief were streaming down my face and I realized something monumental: I love myself.

Looking back at this profound, self-forgiving experience, I now believe it was another epiphany. By forgiving myself, I truly opened the floodgates to allow waves of love to sweep away my feelings of inadequacy.

I use this mechanism for restoring and rebuilding my self-worth preventively, as a daily meditation, or reactively to soothe old wounds that are reopened during the day. I personally have had great success by reading this meditation each morning when I wake up and every night before I go to sleep. Not only does it remind me to forgive myself, but also to be compassionate and accepting of myself. Self-acceptance seems to be the natural by-product of practicing self-forgiveness.

By whole-heartedly accepting myself, even for just a moment, I reinforced my feelings of worthiness. All of us can learn that by being gentle with ourselves when we make mistakes instead of criticizing, we help prevent our fall back into a state of self-loathing. This is self-compassion, and like self-forgiveness and self-acceptance, it is a steppingstone toward self-love. "Self-compassion entails being warm and understanding toward ourselves when we suffer, fail, or feel inadequate, rather than ignoring our pain or flagellating ourselves with self-criticism," said researcher Kristen Neff on www.selfcompassion.org. Once I understood self-compassion, I realized how harsh I had been on myself for most of this life. As previously mentioned in The Perfect Judge chapter, my striving for perfectionism led to the constant failure to reach my unrealistic and unattainable goals. And every time I failed, I chastised myself for not being good enough. Going forward, it is my intention to replace my perfectionism with the more self-compassionate expectation of reasonable thoroughness.

Furthermore, it's very important for me to remember that every time I catch myself judging and not accepting others, it is because I am still judging and not accepting myself. My experience has taught me that until I fully accept myself, I won't be able to fully accept others.

Vulnerability

We cultivate love when we allow our most
vulnerable and powerful selves to be deeply
seen and known, and when we honor the
spiritual connection that grows from that
offering with trust, respect, kindness and
affection. -Brené Brown

As far back as I can remember I was a relatively happy child.
In grade school I was very popular, and most years, I was
the fastest, strongest and most athletic kid in my class. I
was almost always the captain, and if I wasn't, I was always
chosen first for teams. I genuinely felt worthy!

All of this dramatically changed when I entered middle school.
During the summer break, it seemed as though most of the
other kids grew six inches in height, had voice changes and
almost all became faster, stronger and more athletic than I.
Now, for the first time, I was on the other side of the fence.
I was a twerp! Girls towered over me and made fun of my
diminished height and often referred to me as Shrimp or
Midget. And to make matters worse, this was the year that
boys had to take showers together after gym class. Oh my God!

My puberty was about 18 months behind most of the
other kids, and of the 20 boys in the class, there were only

about three of us that didn't have "hair down there." This quickly became common knowledge, and eventually the girls even found out. Subsequently, they added Baldy to the list of demeaning names they used to describe me. For two miserable years I was bullied, harassed, demeaned and treated with complete and utter disdain!

This is the where, when, how and why behind my low self-worth and shame; sharing this with the world is vulnerability!

To me, vulnerability is being an open book and wearing my heart on my sleeve, sharing my deepest insecurities with others in an effort to help myself and others realize that we are not alone in our suffering. In a relationship, vulnerability lays the groundwork for intimacy. When one partner shares his or her insecurities, it often creates a safe space for the other partner to do the same.

In this book I am your partner, and I am sharing with you the most intimate details of my life in an effort to create a safe space for you to do the same. I hope you follow my lead.

The Letting Go Chronicles

The following journal entries portray the intimate details of my deep and mystical exploration of Consciousness Archaeology. They reflect the emotions and intuitions I uncovered and the modalities I used to process them. These revelations ultimately led to the creation of mechanisms that have significantly impacted the evolution of my consciousness.

June 8, 2014

For the last few years, I have diligently practiced The Letting Go Mechanism every time an acute feeling or sensation of negative energy arose within my conscious awareness. So far the results have been fabulous! I have substantially reduced the intense feelings of fear, anxiety and stress, as a large percentage of the negative energy behind them has dissipated.

Subsequently, I started to get lulled into a false sense of security, feeling that this major transformation was going to be much easier than earlier anticipated. I began to think that all I had to do was let go of the acute negative feelings as they arose, and presto, I would be just fine: simple, practical and relatively pain free.

Then yesterday arrived with a rude awakening, as I awoke with a generally uncomfortable feeling that something was wrong or off-kilter. No matter how hard I tried, I couldn't figure out what was triggering it or how to let it go. I didn't feel any acute negative sensations arising, but I did feel frustrated and irritated by everything and everyone. I had the attitude of "Who cares" and "Whatever," and felt mildly depressed for no apparent reason.

It wasn't until today that I finally realized that this subtle, chronic angst has been occurring periodically throughout most of my adult life.

June 10, 2014

Once again, I'm noticing and experiencing subtle, chronic angst and wondering how to pinpoint the source of this discomfort. It's easy to identify and let go of the acute emotion of anxiety that feels like butterflies in my stomach or anger tightening my chest, but how do I let go of a feeling that seems to permeate my entire being?

There are many different life situations that seem to perpetuate these uncomfortable feelings. Discord with family, partners or friends, financial pressures and concerns about our physical, mental and spiritual health all seem to linger in our sub-conscious. These realizations facilitated my creation of the following journaling exercise, which has been very helpful at finding and rectifying most of the circumstances that trigger my anguish.

The Subtle, Chronic Angst Journaling Mechanism

I begin by writing down on a piece of paper all of the life situations that I am presently aware of that may be at the root of my discomfort. I then ask myself if there is anything humanly possible that I can do to lessen any of these burdens. After each specific situation, I list all possible strategies and realistic action steps that I could use to improve the situation, and then, with courage, I promptly and whole-heartedly act upon them.

Once I have done everything humanly possible to rectify these issues, I accept that there is nothing more I can presently resolve, and that unfortunately, some of these situations must remain unresolved for the time being.

I complete this exercise by shredding the journal papers into small pieces and releasing them into the air at the beach, in the woods, or into a fire. This release provides me with a unique sense of catharsis.

June 15, 2014

I think I may be on to something here! Our Inner-Teacher communicates to our Soul through emotions and intuitions, and we communicate back through journaling. And in doing so, we are essentially guiding the person with handwritten, step-by-step instructions. In some mystical way, journaling bridges the gap between the person and the Soul.

June 19, 2014

The Letting Go Mechanism truly is a life saver! It absolutely saved my life. For 30 years I suffered from chronic anxiety. It was so bad that I eventually needed to go on Paxil just to function. Fortunately, Paxil settled me down and enabled me to calmly and clearly examine my lifetime of emotional peaks and valleys.

Before Paxil, in addition to anxiety, I also experienced chronic and acute episodes of anger. As far back as I can remember I had frequent tantrums, and countless times during these outbursts I punched walls and broke things. One time I even shattered the windshield of my mom's car after punching it from the inside. If I had to choose one word that best described me during this phase of my life, it would be RAGE!

According to Gary Zukav, "All hostility originates in fear. And anger is the agony of believing that you are not capable of being understood, and that you are not worthy of being understood" (131).

Zukav's revelation helped me to finally understand that this anger could primarily be a reaction to the shame that I experienced from being bullied in middle school. Soon after this bullying began, I started bullying others. From 9th to 12th grade I was in more than 20 fist fights, and most of them I instigated and brutally finished. And as hard as it may seem to believe, beating someone to a bloody pulp actually brought me momentary relief from my anguish.

Fortunately, letting go has given me back control over this anger and shame. Hostile feelings still come up, but every time they do, I pause and remember to let them go.

The Letting Go Mechanism is so simple and practical that it almost doesn't seem possible or real. Trust me, the results are very real, and they have helped me to transform from a very anxious, angry man into the loving, caring individual that I am today.

Now that I have been practicing letting go for years, I have noticed that harmless thoughts are beginning to replace the harmful feelings that used to arise whenever my buttons were pushed, and harmless thoughts are a piece of cake!

June 22, 2014

Going for a quiet walk in nature is a letting go mechanism in and of itself. I utilize these walks whenever I sense the presence of discomfort or unease. This feeling often arises at lunchtime when I get completely caught up with my daily work and personal responsibilities. In this moment, the distraction of tasks I still have to complete is no longer present, and in the lull that remains, I'm left with just me and my thoughts. Occasionally, these thoughts are accompanied by boredom or depression.

When these uncomfortable feelings arise, I know it's time for a "Letting Go" walk. Usually, halfway through this walk, I feel relaxed and very grateful for the Divine gift of this free time: the time to just be and enjoy the solitude of nature, the time for reflection and quiet contemplation, and the time to listen for intuitive guidance from my Inner-Teacher.

I also use other forms of letting go, such as taking drives through the country, bicycling, running, sitting meditation -- anything that creates a comfortable setting for surrendering the uncomfortable energy behind my emotions.

June 29, 2014

Just when I thought I had a mechanism for every situation, this weekend brought a new twist. For reasons unbeknownst to me, I awoke yesterday morning feeling anxious. I spent the entire day by myself, writing and editing this book. I was in business mode with the "Git-er done" attitude, but just under the surface, a subtle anxiety remained. Off and on throughout the day I stopped what I was doing and desperately tried to pinpoint the source of my discomfort. No matter which mechanism I used, I simply couldn't get to the root of my unease. Subsequently, I ended up going to bed distracted by unresolved issues.

Needless to say, I awoke this morning in the same state. The slight but persistent anxiety reminded me of my pre-Paxil days many years ago. After a second unsuccessful attempt at The Subtle, Chronic Angst Journaling Mechanism, I finally gave up, declaring that no matter what I did or said, I was not going to figure this one out. Without realizing it, by throwing in the towel, I inadvertently let go of the strong desire to discover the root of my problem and began to feel the slightest bit of relief. Letting go of this desire, which was exacerbating my anxiety, allowed me to breathe and start to relax for the first time in two days.

Upon reflection, I was reminded that I may not always be able to find the exact source of my angst and that is ok.

June 30, 2014

By letting go of the desire to actively locate the source of my angst, I am essentially surrendering control. When I closely examine control, it becomes obvious that I spend most of my waking hours trying to control everything and everybody. First, I am constantly trying to create the perfect environment for myself to evolve and when this doesn't always materialize, I become dumbfounded. What do you mean I can't control the pace of my evolution? Secondly, I attempt to persuade others to do things my way and if they don't, it feels as if something must clearly be very wrong with them.

Looking back, I realized that I have spent my entire life trying to control the outcome of my marriage, my career, the lives of my children and now the life of my new partner. Furthermore, being entrepreneurial and leadership-driven seems to intensify these controlling tendencies. The significant success of my professional life has clearly proven that my decision-making skills are top notch. The same could be said for the success of my spiritual journey, as I have evolved from the depths of despair to the consistent peaceful existence that I cherish today. These thoughts create the illusion that I have my shit together and "you all" damn-well better listen to my advice, as I clearly know what is best for you!

So, how does one let go of this powerful desire to control? Desire is a feeling, and like any other feeling or emotion, we have a mechanism for letting it go: The Letting Go Mechanism.

July 2, 2014

What exactly does it mean when we have a chronic desire for our lives to be different? In most cases it indicates that we are unsatisfied with ourselves. This dissatisfaction often leads us to need external validation of our worthiness. Some get this validation by achieving illustrious careers, owning fancy homes and luxury cars or possessing trophy spouses. Unfortunately, these external rewards can bring only a temporary sense of pleasure in the form of false pride.

Another unhealthy manifestation of desire is our perpetual craving for others to be exactly like we are -- to have all of the same interests, preferences and physical, emotional and spiritual attributes. Most importantly, these clones would whole-heartedly agree with everything that we said or did. Desire gives rise to the secret yearning for a person who would constantly approve of us and therefore validate our worthiness.

The truth is that neither of these, nor any other linear support system, is going to provide lasting satisfaction and certainly not contentment.

Then what is the magical elixir? GRATITUDE!!!!!

Melody Beattie offers this beautiful tribute: "Gratitude unlocks the fullness of life. It turns what we have into enough, and more. It turns denial into acceptance, chaos to order, confusion to clarity. It can turn a meal into a feast, a house into a home, a stranger into a friend."

Gratitude reminds us that joy originates from within, not from frivolous external pleasures. At the end of book two, we will dive much deeper into gratitude and many other fine virtues!

Book Two

Intentionally Moving
Toward the Light

*Dear Universe: Will I ever
become enlightened?
"Yes, no, both and neither." (347)*

Introduction

Every person has a unique personality that displays a variety of different attributes, and each Soul resides at a specific level of consciousness or maturity. This level of maturity is based on the Soul's proximity to the light or the dark. How can the Soul intentionally move toward the light? By practicing The Mechanism of Transformation.

The Mechanism of Transformation is a six-step spiritual maturation process:

Recognition: Noticing or being aware of emotions and intuitions as they arise; mindfulness.

Acknowledgment: Understanding and accepting that positive reactions to these emotions and intuitions trigger trust (light) and negative reactions trigger doubt (dark); affirmation.

Intention: Purposely moving toward the light whenever possible; impulsion.

Attention: The concentration of the mind on the furtherance of the intention; awareness.

Implementation: The action step of following through with the intention of moving toward the light; execution.

Manifestation: The evolution of consciousness and spiritual maturity; materialization.

Every time a feeling or emotion arises within our conscious awareness, we recognize its presence, acknowledge the sensation and then ask the Universe to guide our intention. Once our intention is created, we shall diligently focus our attention on its furtherance through implementation, which ultimately leads to its manifestation.

We may not always be able to control our reactions to situations, but we certainly can always have the intention to react from a place of love. Going forward, it shall be our intention to shift from being unconsciously controlled by fearful emotions to consciously choosing to act on love-centered intuitions.

Our intentions create our experiences. The more attention that we direct toward fulfilling our intention, the more likely it will be implemented and henceforth manifested into our lives.

The Transformation Chronicles

The following journal entries exemplify my journey through the transformation process and continue in the Questions for the Universe chapter that follows.

July 24, 2014

The ebbs and flows of this earth-life experience occasionally bring me to my knees to plead with the Universe to please help me to find my way! In this humble state of surrender, I am reminded of my favorite quotation about courage by Mary Anne Radmacher, who said, "Courage doesn't always roar. Sometimes courage is the little voice at the end of the day that says I'll try again tomorrow."

These words bring tears to my eyes and peace to my heart. They remind me to be self-compassionate and gentle with myself, as I can't always roar like a lion and passionately blaze my trail. Sometimes I need to rest and just be, as a respite may be exactly what the Universe ordered.

When I asked the Universe to "Please help me to find my way," the answer that arose was to be patient and calmly endure hardship, pain or delay and to demonstrate perseverance, restraint and determination.

Recognizing that life has ups and downs and acknowledging that these ebbs and flows often lead to a roller coaster ride of emotions are the first two steps on the path of transformation.

July 25, 2014

I can be very judgmental, and when I act like this I have recognized and acknowledged that I usually hurt another person's feelings. Knowing I have hurt someone triggers my guilt, shame and remorse. Going forward, it is my intention to replace this condemnation with understanding and appreciation.

July 27, 2014

My occasional inability to get along well with others often stems from intolerance, as my unwillingness or refusal to respect contrary opinions or beliefs triggers discord. Whenever this disharmony arises, it becomes obvious that I am moving away from the light and not honoring the virtue of tolerance. What exactly is tolerance? My original interpretation was: open-mindedness to ideas, opinions and practices that differ from one's own; the absence of prejudice; and having a live-and-let-live attitude.

While reflecting on this definition, "honor diversity" bubbled up as an intuitive thought. How can diversity be blended into tolerance? The following by Hong Tran offers this suggestion: "The concept of diversity encompasses acceptance and respect. It is about understanding each other and moving beyond simple tolerance to embracing and celebrating the rich dimensions of diversity contained within each individual."

Going forward and moving toward the light, it is my intention to expand my interpretation of tolerance to include recognizing, acknowledging and honoring the innate brilliance, vibrancy and radiance in others, and by doing so, I shall be practicing reverence.

According to Gary Zukav, "Reverence is seeing beyond the outer shell of appearance to the essence within it. Reverence is connecting with the true power and essence of what a person is or a thing is. It is a holy perception. It is recognizing personalities as Earth suits and shifting your attention away from the Earth suit to what is wearing it. That is the soul. Reverence is accepting that all Life is, in and of itself, sacred" (262).

July 30, 2014

Karma:

Everything that we say or do, either comes back to bite us in the ass or kiss us on the cheek. That's Karma! When we move toward the light, the light naturally moves toward us, and conversely, when we move toward the dark, the dark naturally does the same.

July 31, 2014

T.G.I.N.

Thank God it's now!

By intentionally moving toward the light, every day is the best day of our lives, as each day we are slightly more evolved, and with that maturity an increased peace of mind naturally follows.

August 3, 2014

When I awoke this morning, I got on my knees, put my hands together and said the following: Thank you for this experience; I surrender this life and this will to Thee. Please help me to find my way.

Instantaneously, the Universe spoke the following back to me:

You are to dedicate the rest of this earth-life experience to compassion: a deep empathy that gives rise to an active desire to alleviate the suffering of others by wrapping them in a safe, nurturing blanket of unconditional love and fostering an environment that is conducive for self-validation of their innate beauty, perfection and worthiness. And don't forget that the ability to have compassion for others starts with showing compassion for yourself. This devotion shall be embodied through your daily interactions with others and, on a much grander scale, through your writings. I shall continue to guide you through this transformation process and will do so through a question and answer format.

Questions for the Universe

August 4, 2014

Q: What does it mean to truly surrender and how is it done?

A: Surrendering is throwing in the towel or waving the white flag. Spiritually, surrendering is giving up control of your life and recognizing and acknowledging that a power greater than you is driving the bus. This often starts with the simple request of "Please help me to find my way." As soon as this appeal is expressed, it shall become intuitively known to you that I, The Universe, have always been there, helping you to find your way. You just didn't fully realize it.

August 5, 2014

Q: What does the feeling of anger teach me?

A: It teaches you that you are resisting the circumstances that are unfolding in the present moment and that your desire to control the outcome is not being fulfilled. Always remember that contentment is nothing more than a complete absence of resistance to what is.

Q: What does the feeling of lust teach me?

A: It reminds you that sexual desire is very powerful and must be kept in check, and like any other desire, it teaches you that true fulfillment can only come from within, not from transitory external stimulation. And lastly, be grateful for what you have, not envious for what you have not.

August 6, 2014

Q: If others aren't as organized, disciplined and aware as I am, does that mean that they are flawed?

A: No, it simply means that they are different than you. There is no such thing as flawed. Each person has different interests and different things that they excel in.

August 8, 2014

Q: How do I stop judging the attributes of others?

A: By practicing reverence and having the intention to see through their transitory person and personality and directly view their eternal Soul in all of its splendor and beauty.

Q: How do I stop judging my own attributes?

A: By practicing reverence and having the intention to see through your transitory person and personality and directly view your eternal Soul in all of its splendor and beauty.

August 11, 2014

Q: What is the purpose of a spiritual partnership?

A: The purpose of each Soul's earth-life experience is to evolve and mature. By experiencing the vicissitudes and joys of life, the Soul recognizes and acknowledges which tendencies pull it closer to the light or closer to the dark. Each Soul's purpose in a spiritual partnership is to foster the evolution of the other Soul's maturity by wrapping him or her in a safe, nurturing blanket of unconditional love. A partner understands that Souls will occasionally struggle with the human affliction of low self-worth. It is the partner's responsibility to help create the environment that will allow the other Soul to self-validate his or her own worthiness.

Q: Is that the only purpose for the spiritual partnership?

A: The interplay and synergy of a spiritual partnership also brings to the surface all of the dark attributes that are obstructing each Soul's movement toward the light and all of the light attributes that are supporting each Soul's movement away from the dark. These vicissitudes and joys create an abundance of opportunities for Soul maturity.

August 14, 2014

Q: How can a preconceived notion regarding the reason why someone is acting a certain way be recontexualized?

A: By having the intention to understand the motivation behind the trait that you find unacceptable, you are better able to see the situation from a non-judgmental perspective. Let's use procrastination as an example. Without understanding, procrastination could be viewed as a form of laziness, inefficiency, ineptness or irresponsibility. However, the truth about why people procrastinate is very simple. According to Phil Stutz and Barry Michels from the Greatist blog, "The list of things we can procrastinate about is endless, but the list of reasons why we procrastinate is not. We avoid every task for the same reason: Taking action will cause us a certain amount of pain."

Once you understand that someone is exhibiting fear of facing his or pain, not incompetence, you are better able to shift your focus to compassion.

Q: How does one overcome procrastination?

A: By having the intention and courage to face one's pain.

Q: What steps can be taken to face this pain?

A: Through journaling, first recognize by writing down on a piece of paper all of the daunting tasks that are on your mental "to do" list. Then acknowledge that this unfinished business is weighing very heavily on your mind. The next step is to create the intention to do whatever it takes to accomplish these goals and set up a timetable for implementation. After each item, designate whether it can be accomplished immediately, within a week, month or any other amount of time that is realistic and acceptable for each situation. And last but not least: Git er done! As each task is implemented, pain is lessened, fear is diminished and peace of mind begins to manifest.

Q: What finally triggers the procrastinator to act?

A: When the pain of not following through with a task exceeds the pain of following through.

August 15, 2014

Q: Why are people so afraid to face their pain?

A: Because experiencing pain takes them out of their comfort zone.

Q: What is at the root of this pain?

A: Embarrassment, fear, humiliation or shame. By facing pain, they are reminded of the possibility that they may possess inadequacies and be unworthy. Avoidance allows them to remain in denial and safely in their comfort zones.

Q: How can I help someone who seems to be unable to face his or her fears?

A: By remembering that everybody evolves at their own pace and that your only responsibility is to be compassionate.

Q: Do you have any helpful reminders?

A: Each morning, have the intention to recite the following: "Please help me to find my way and allow everyone else to find theirs."

Q: That sounds like "Live and Let Live?"

A: Precisely.

August 16, 2014

Q: What can I do to stop feeling like a bad dog?

A: Stop acting like a bad dog.

Q: What do you mean?

A: Every time that you have been arrogant, judgmental, spiteful or condemning, you naturally played the role of bad dog and therefore felt like one because shame for what you have done leads to this feeling.

Q: What is the most basic and simple reminder that I could use to stop exhibiting these vices?

A: Be nice, feel good! Every time that you are nice, you are reinforcing your goodness and moving toward the light and every time that you are rude, you are reinforcing your arrogance and moving toward the dark.

Q: But why do I sometimes feel like a bad dog even when I haven't been acting like one?

A: There are many different variations of shame. One is situation-driven acute shame that abruptly surfaces as an after effect of exhibiting bad dog behavior. Another type of shame is more chronic and subtle and seems to linger just below the surface of your being.

Q: What causes this subtle, chronic shame?

A: Most often, this shame develops in childhood, either from a particular parenting style or bullying experiences in the school setting. And in some cases, people are born into this lifetime with the karmic predisposition for shame.

Q: Is there any way to alleviate a lifelong affliction of subtle, chronic shame?

A: Dr. Marc Miller says "Most people feel shame about feeling shame. As a result shame is rarely acknowledged to others, or even to oneself." Therefore, the first step in alleviating subtle, chronic shame is to recognize its presence and acknowledge that it may have been unknowingly encumbering you for most of your life.

August 18, 2014

Q: What are some ways to alleviate depression?

A: The same way that you alleviate shame, angst, anxiety and all other forms of discomfort.

Q: Please refresh my memory.

A: A very helpful and illuminating exercise is to write down on a piece of paper all of your unresolved issues or areas of discomfort that you believe are causing your depression. Once you feel that your list is all-inclusive, follow through with the remainder of the steps in The Subtle, Chronic Angst Journaling Mechanism.

Q: How does this help?

A: It reduces the fear of the unknown. Through courageously honest journaling, you will see exactly what is at the root of your discomfort. Once you recognize the source and acknowledge that this may be triggering your depression, you can begin the letting go practice by creating the intention to take all possible action steps necessary to alleviate this discomfort.

August 19, 2014

Q: Please refresh my memory again: What is the antidote for judgmentalism?

A: Understanding. By having the intention to uncover the motivation behind someone's actions, you will better understand why people act the way they do. Understanding dissolves judgment and lays the groundwork for acceptance and compassion.

Q: Ok, then help me to understand people's motivation behind enabling others, especially their own children?

A: It's usually out of fear of being rejected or possibly abandoned or estranged. There is a very fine line between loving support and enabling.

Q: What triggers their fear of rejection?

A: For them, rejection announces to the world and themselves that they are unworthy. Enabling provides them with a false sense of worthiness and momentary escape from their shame; it keeps their secret safe.

Q: What is the difference between enabling and allowing?

A: Enabling temporarily delays the other's inevitable karma and helps the enabler to avoid shame. Allowing consequences to naturally unfold brings both of their destinies to the forefront.

August 20, 2014

Q: How are the labels *undisciplined, unreliable, oblivious* and *ignorant* viewed through the lens of understanding?

A: Let's take one at a time, starting with *undisciplined.* Discipline is not an all-or-nothing proposition. Most people are disciplined about some things and undisciplined about others. Everyone has different priorities and their top priorities get the majority of their attention.

Q: Why are people unreliable?

A: People can be forgetful and this oftentimes is misinterpreted as lack of reliability. Some people forget things because they have weak memories others forget because they unknowingly repress their uncomfortable thoughts.

Q: Is obliviousness also because of forgetfulness?

A: In some cases, forgetfulness is behind someone's perceived lack of awareness, but in most cases, people simply don't see everything that is going on around them. Many are distracted by the multitude of daily life responsibilities; others get bogged down in daydream-like states that take them away from the present moment.

Q: Couldn't ignorance be viewed through the same lens?

A: Through a similar lens, but naïveté is a kinder way to view ignorance.

Q: How would you define naïveté?

A: As having or showing a lack of experience, judgment, or information. Naive people are willing to believe or trust too readily, especially without proper or adequate evidence. The word *gullible* is sometimes appropriate.

That is loving! Once again, understanding the motivation behind people's actions sheds light on why they might be acting the way they are. Therefore, understanding could be viewed as the lens of unconditional love.

August 21, 2014

The insight you provided me yesterday was invaluable, and it created the intention for me to view all aspects of human behavior through this new lens. Just to recap yesterday: Understanding is the lens of unconditional love and through that lens the following initial perceptions could be recontexualized as noted below. I added in a few extra ones after experiencing some new opportunities later in the day.

Unreliable: Occasionally forgetful.

Ignorant: Exhibiting a naive moment.

Undisciplined: Uncommitted to that particular goal.

Oblivious: Momentarily unaware.

Unreasonable: Reasonably human.

Emotionally incapacitated or overwhelmed: In need of extra love.

Unstable: In need of support.

Unavailable or disconnected: In need of a safe space to adjust, adapt and reconnect.

Q: Do you agree?

A: Freeman, your recontexualizations are spot on!

August 22, 2014

Q: What about when someone seems to be rejecting me? How is that viewed through the lens of understanding?

A: Quite often, people become disconnected when their shame is triggered, and this unavailability could be perceived as their rejection of you. However, more than likely, they are really rejecting themselves, as shame triggers their sensation of low self-worth. So, instead of taking it personally, reach out to them compassionately and do whatever you can to ease their pain.

Q: Could there be other reasons?

A: From another perspective, their rejecting of themselves could be mirroring back to you the fact that you are simultaneously rejecting yourself. As previously mentioned, Carl Jung stated that "Everything that irritates us about others can lead us to an understanding of ourselves." That could explain the discomfort that one feels when another person is exhibiting his or her discomfort.

Q: Why do I feel so uncomfortable around people when they display an inferiority complex?

A: Because it mirrors back to you the reality that you also occasionally display an inferiority complex.

Q: So, the concept of mirroring manifests in many different ways?

A: Indeed.

August 23, 2014

Q: Why do most people seem to be in the constant pursuit of happiness?

A: Because each person enters the earth-life experience with the innate proclivity to strive for happiness.

Q: Are you saying that each person's primary intention is to do everything humanly possible to feel good?

A: Basically yes, but more specifically, the motivation behind every human intention is to achieve contentment.

Q: How is contentment different from happiness?

A: According to Michael Graham, "Contentment may be considered as synonymous with happiness, but is more basic or prior to happiness that can be derived from outer achievement or self-improvement. For this reason, contentment is simply a way of accepting one's life state and being grateful or happy with it."

Q: Is that the same as joy?

A: Joy is the non-verbal expression of contentment.

August 25, 2014

Q: Do I need to spend the rest of my life learning more about spirituality in order to evolve?

A: Absolutely not. There comes a time when you will realize that you have learned all you need to know about spirituality. Once this occurs, the process of unlearning can begin. Unlearning starts with humility: the acknowledgment that you know absolutely nothing for certain. Once accepted, this path of belieflessness shall trigger you to reexamine and then recontexualize every opinion and belief that arises within your conscious awareness.

Q: What types of opinions and beliefs are you referring to?

A: Every time that you evaluate or judge someone or something as right or wrong or good or bad, you are expressing an opinion or belief.

Q: Can you provide a few more examples?

A: Whenever you make a declarative statement, you are sharing your viewpoint. On the path of belieflessness, all ideas are expressed in a tentative or provisional way.

Q: What are the benefits of belieflessness?

A: Once you begin to know nothing for certain, you become open to viewing things as they actually are.

Q: How are things, actually?

A: In actuality, the concept of cause and effect isn't as simple as it first appears to be. What is actually occurring isn't always based solely on one current event; instead, actuality is the expression of all potentiality that has accumulated during an entire lifetime or several lifetimes.

Q: How is that helpful for unlearning?

A: By not jumping to conclusions, you are better able to give yourself and others the benefit of the doubt. When accusing someone or yourself of some misdeed, you could instead ask what triggered the response and what is the motivation behind this behavior? Quite often, you will find out that your preconceived notions and conditioned thoughts were totally inaccurate.

Q: What happens once the unlearning process is complete?

A: Contentment and peace of mind gently settles in and nourishes your being. Some refer to this as enlightenment.

August 26, 2014

Q: What does enlightenment feel like?

A: It feels like a very deep sense of knowing nothing for certain, going with the flow and having a complete absence of resistance to what is, being mystically stricken with the inability to form an opinion or judgment about anything, and a total surrender or letting go of all preconceived notions and conditioned thoughts.

Q: That sounds like belieflessness?

A: It is.

August 27, 2014

Q: What is a synonym for belieflessness?

A: Freedom.

Q: Can you define freedom in this context please?

A: Freedom from judgment, criticism, condemnation and disdain; freedom to love, cherish, savor and fully experience joy.

Mmmmm...freedom to move away from the dark and freedom to move toward the light.

August 31, 2014

Q: What is the fastest way to enlightenment?

A: Put on a pair of enlightened spectacles and never take them off.

Q: What the heck are enlightened spectacles?

A: There are two primary paths to Peace: the path through the mind and the path through the heart. A healthy blend of the two often sets the stage for one to be pulled through the final doorway. These paths could be viewed as the two lenses of the enlightened spectacles. The first lens portrays everything through unconditional love and the second lens portrays everything through belieflessness.

September 2, 2014

Q: What else can you tell me about Souls?

A: There are young Souls, old Souls and everything in between Souls. All of these Souls have an aura. Young or immature Souls have an underdeveloped or weak aura, and old or mature Souls have a highly developed, powerful aura.

As previously discussed, each person enters the world in a state of pure innocence; preconceived notions and conditioned thoughts do not exist. As nurture and nature take its toll, the person eventually gets bogged down with learned beliefs and opinions. It is the Soul's job to help the person unlearn all of this conditioning; by doing so, the person and the Soul simultaneously evolve. The more mature the Soul is, the greater the aura and influence that it has on the person.

Q: Does that mean that old Souls are better than young Souls?

A: No, they are just more mature. Souls are like trees. As time goes by they both grow and mature. Trees evolve from seedlings to saplings to small trees to medium trees to fully-grown trees. During this entire evolution process they are always perfect and complete. However, oftentimes trees struggle and need extra care, but at no point in time are they ever any better than they were at any other point in time, nor are they any better than any other tree.

September 3, 2014

Q: Even after years of diligent and tenacious spiritual work, I still occasionally exhibit arrogance, narcissism, false pride and entitlement. Is it ever possible to completely eliminate these traits from the personality?

A: As hard as you, the Soul, try to change the person, the truth is that trying to change the personality is no different from trying to change the height of the body. The general traits of the personality are born and die with the body.

Q: Can I control the person's thoughts?

A: Not a chance. The person's thoughts arise of their own volition and are therefore independent of and out of the Soul's control.

Q: Is there any way to manage the person's emotions?

A: Fortunately, yes you can.

Q: How exactly is that management implemented?

A: There are many different strategies for reducing emotional discomfort, but therapy and medication are the two most frequently utilized.

Q: I've benefitted greatly from therapy and medication and strongly encourage others to consider these strategies. However, in some cases, therapy and medication alone are not capable of providing complete relief. Could you suggest an alternative approach?

A: The Letting Go Mechanism is an extremely effective means of eliminating emotional discomfort. Once an emotion is surrendered, the negative energy behind it lessens, and after practicing "Letting Go" for a period of time, harmful emotions are eventually replaced by harmless thoughts.

Q: Will letting go of negative emotions have any effect on my person's arrogance, narcissism, false pride and entitlement?

A: Yes and no. By significantly reducing negative energy, the person will be more receptive to the Soul's loving influence of humility. Humility is like a natural, spiritual medication that mystically buffers some of the personality's rough edges.

Q: Is humility the only natural, spiritual medication available?

A: There are countless other spiritual remedies, but my other three favorites are gratitude, patience and compassion.

Q: Can you tell me which other virtues you highly value?

A: Honesty, integrity, tolerance, graciousness, acceptance, forgiveness, benevolence and understanding round out my top twelve.

Q: So, what you are saying is that I cannot completely change the personality, but I can positively influence the person's general manner of being?

A: That's what I'm saying.

October 9, 2014

Q: What is consciousness?

A: Consciousness is the person's physical expression of the Soul's level of maturity.

Q: Is consciousness linear or non-linear?

A: Consciousness is non-linear, but it is linearly expressed in the person as his or her demeanor.

Q: What types of demeanor are you referring to?

A: Consciousness can be expressed as a full spectrum of demeanors including anger, pride, love, grief, contentment, shame, courage, apathy, desire and joy.

Q: What dictates this demeanor?

A: The Soul's level of maturity.

Q: Is this demeanor changeable?

A: Yes, as the Soul matures, the person's demeanor becomes more positive and loving.

October 10, 2014

Q: Is it possible to become more aware?

A: Yes and no. There are two types of awareness: linear perception and non-linear, intuitive comprehension. Perception is an aspect of intellect and therefore unchangeable, but intuitive comprehension increases as the Soul's level of consciousness rises.

Q: Does the same hold true for memory?

A: Yes. Linear memory, or memory of the mind, is also an unchanging aspect of intellect; however, non-linear memory, or memory of the heart, is an aspect of ever-evolving consciousness, and therefore expandable.

Q: So, I cannot become smarter, but I can become more aware?

A: Exactly.

Q: How exactly does that happen?

A: By unlearning all beliefs, you are removing the obstructions that were previously blocking intuition from entering your conscious awareness.

Q: What is intuition?

A: Intuition is wisdom from the Universe.

Q: Why doesn't intuition increase my intellect?

A: Your intellect, like your personality, is pre-determined at birth, and is therefore unchangeable.

Q: I still don't believe that intellect is fixed. Can you prove it?

A: Before you evolved to your present state of awareness, you were unable to understand calculus, you struggled with assembling and setting up electronic devices, and you could never remember detailed, step-by-step directions that were given to you verbally. Has any of this changed over the years of your spiritual education?

Hmmmm….very interesting! The truth is that I still struggle with those and many other linear intellectual challenges.

October 13, 2014

Q: What morning prayer do you suggest?

A: I suggest that you stay with what has worked so well for you thus far: "Thank you for this experience. Please help me to find my way and to have patience, trust and faith that you shall continue to provide me with everything that I need, exactly when I need it."

Mmmmm...that prayer has brought me such comfort. It reduces my impatient seeking and striving for immediate answers for everything. When I breathe, relax and listen, the way eventually uncovers itself.

October 15, 2014

Q: How else can I be a kinder person?

A: By having the intention to learn more about the virtues and unlearn more of the vices. The next chapter shall assist you with this next stage of your journey.

Virtue and Vice

Many years ago I was a self-centered, egotistical, judgmental know-it-all. Needless to say, I was not very well-liked or respected. I chalked this behavior off to: "This is just who I am; take it or leave it. It's not as if I can change or anything!"

It wasn't until I started reading self-improvement books in the mid-90s that I discovered that change is possible (more about this later). I also realized that if I were just a little bit nicer, less arrogant, egotistical and judgmental, people would start to like and respect me a little bit more.

These realizations led to a relentless 10-year reading frenzy. During this time, I created a list of all the positive attributes that each author consistently mentioned, and then went through years of my notes and tabulated which ones appeared most often. Twelve of these attributes stood out head and shoulders above the rest, and I sensed that the term virtue was the best way to classify these sacred words. These virtues are understanding, honesty, humility, forgiveness, acceptance, patience, tolerance, gratitude, graciousness, benevolence, compassion and integrity.

Intentionally moving toward the light starts with the intention to practice and embody these virtues. When our behavior is virtuous, we are moving toward the light, and when our behavior is vice-centered, we are moving toward the dark. Virtues and vices exemplify either fear (dark) or love (light). It's important to recognize and acknowledge the physical sensations we experience when either the light or the dark present themselves. Notice that whenever love arises, the Soul feels nourished and the person feels light and at ease, and whenever fear arises, the Soul feels malnourished and the person feels dark and diseased.

The virtues and vices listed below are guideposts along the path. May we have the intention to embrace the virtues and the inner-joy that arises, but also give attention to the sorrow that ensues when we exhibit the vices.

Understanding: Wisdom, awareness, perspective and intuition; mindfulness; the ability to comprehend one's own and others' feelings, attitude and points of view; empathy.

-Obliviousness, Apathy

The embodiment of understanding develops through awareness and intuition. The evolution of consciousness starts with the understanding that spiritual maturity is indeed possible. Attempting to evolve without understanding is like trying to drive a car without gas. Understanding enables us to shift from the emotional participant or experiencer of life to the emotionless witness-observer. And most importantly, understanding leads us back to the Divine realization that we are not a transitory person and that we are the eternal Soul.

Honesty: Truthfulness, sincerity and self-knowledge; communicating and acting authentically with oneself and others.

-Dishonesty, Inauthenticity

The practice of self-honesty is to fearlessly face our perceived inadequacies by tenaciously digging through our own rubble to uncover our innate perfection and completeness. Self-honesty reveals all of the obstacles that are obscuring our true worth, and these opinions, beliefs, preconceived notions and conditioned thoughts limit our spiritual maturity.

Humility: Freedom from false pride or arrogance; having an awareness of one's own shortcomings and others' strengths; exhibiting a modest, humble aura; belieflessness.

-Arrogance, False pride, Entitlement

The practice of humility is to intentionally travel down the path of belieflessness by surrendering all opinions, beliefs, preconceived notions and conditioned thoughts and starting with a blank slate. On this humble path, aversions and attractions no longer exist. Declarations of *should have, must be, definitely, obviously, incontestably* and *certainly* won't be found here. Alternatively, speculations like *seems to, might be, could have* and *possibly*, depict the communication style of its travelers.

Humility is also the understanding that our Souls are no better or worse than any other Souls. We all possess a mosaic of attributes that make us *different from* one another, but not *greater* or *less than*.

Forgiveness: A letting go or releasing of resentments; the willingness to move beyond past events, perhaps to reconcile and restore.

-Accusation, Blame, Resentment

The practice of self-forgiveness helps to create the blank slate by lessening the burdens of guilt and remorse and dissolving self-inflicted grudges and harsh criticisms. Self-forgiveness unlocks the door and allows the essence of our wonderful Soul to shine forth. Once our goodness is brought into the light, the darkness of our negative energy is overshadowed. To forgive ourselves is the greatest gift that we can ever bestow.

Acceptance: Acknowledgement of the truth regarding a situation or condition; appreciation and validation of one's own and others' human personalities (even traits we may wish to change); letting go of resistance and denial; absolute cooperation with the inevitable.

-Denial, Resistance, Rejection

The embodiment of self-acceptance enables us to have a complete absence of resistance to our person's human traits including the personality and the characteristics of the body.

Patience: Calm endurance of hardship, pain or delay; demonstrating perseverance, restraint and determination.

-Impatience, Agitation, Striving, Frustration

The embodiment of patience is restraint, determination and a calm endurance of the delay required for spiritual maturity to gradually unfold. Patience is at the heart of our ability to pause and gives us the opportunity to practice The Letting Go Mechanism each time an uncomfortable feeling arises. Patience helps us to build and save relationships and to become great partners, parents, sons or daughters, friends and co-workers.

Tolerance: Open-mindedness to ideas, opinions and practices that differ from one's own; the absence of prejudice and a live-and-let-live attitude; the embracing and celebrating of diversity by recognizing, acknowledging and honoring the innate brilliance, vibrancy and radiance in others; reverence.

-Intolerance, Narrow-mindedness, Prejudice

The embodiment of tolerance is reverence and the honoring of diversity in others. Tolerance reminds us that we are all on this journey together to individually and collectively evolve. Everything that we do or say has profound implications on all humanity. As we evolve, all of the people in the world evolve simultaneously. We truly are one human race. We are humans being…together.

Gratitude: Thankful appreciation for what one has received; showing gratefulness and recognition to others.

-Ingratitude, Desire

The embodiment of gratitude is seeing the beauty in everything, and thoroughly appreciating the simple things in life. Gratitude is not possible until self-forgiveness is practiced and self-acceptance is embodied. The inclination to be gracious, benevolent and compassionate originates as a result of the embodiment of gratitude. Gratitude truly does unlock the fullness of life!

Graciousness: The attribute of being kind to all; politeness, cordiality and good-natured disposition.

-Impoliteness, Pompousness

The practice of graciousness is going out of our way to show our kindness to everyone. Graciousness is the acknowledgement that everybody is perfect and complete and worthy and deserving of our kindness and generosity.

Benevolence: Friendliness, kindness, selflessness and the inclination to be generous; having a love of humankind accompanied by a desire to encourage the happiness of others.

-Selfishness, Greediness, Unkindness

The practice of benevolence is the quiet expression of our generosity. The greatest gift that we can give others is ourselves, our time and undivided attention and appreciation. Benevolence specifically directed toward those who are suffering could be viewed as compassion.

Compassion: A deep empathy that gives rise to an active desire to alleviate the suffering of others by wrapping them in a safe, nurturing blanket of unconditional love; the fostering of an environment that is conducive for self-validation of others' innate beauty, perfection and worthiness.

-Cruelty, Hatred, Indifference

The practice of compassion involves actively seeking out those in need and promptly and gently reaching out to them in an effort to lessen their burdens. We know that we have reached a different level of spiritual maturity once we notice our sense of compassion. Through understanding, patience, forgiveness and graciousness, we become the loving people that we always aspired to be. This leads to our new found ability to benevolently reach out to others. Compassion takes benevolence to a whole new level.

Integrity: Moral consistency of actions, values and principles; honesty in regard to the motivations of one's actions.

-Hypocrisy, Immorality, Inconsistency

The practice of integrity is the consistent expression and embodiment of all virtues.

These 12 virtues methodically woven together form the Divine fabric of unconditional love. Furthermore, they facilitate the evolution of consciousness and the recognition and acknowledgment of our Inner-Genius.

Inner-Genius

Recognized geniuses may be rare, but genius resides within all of us. A primary reason that so many people fail to recognize, and therefore empower their own genius is because in the popular mind, genius is confused with a high IQ. This is a gross misunderstanding, which has arisen from the fact that many celebrated geniuses in the fields of mathematics and physics indeed have high IQs; however, in those fields, the IQ necessary to comprehend the work is a prerequisite. It would be more helpful to see genius as simply an extraordinary high degree of insight in a given area of human activity. –David R. Hawkins

I did not become aware of my Inner-Genius until I was 18 years old. Up until that time, the thought of me being a genius seemed absurd. In elementary and middle school I was an average student, and I despised reading books, as I arrogantly thought that was something that only sissies did. I was much more interested in football, baseball and any other type of rough-and-tumble activity.

In high school, my life took a dramatic turn away from all forms of genius. In 10th grade I was introduced to marijuana, and as soon as I experienced my first high, I knew that I had found my new best friend. Smoking pot immediately took away all of my fears and insecurities and made me feel invincible. Over time, the high of marijuana wasn't enough, and this led to my experimentation with LSD, cocaine, amphetamines and any other drug that someone's parents had in their medicine cabinets. By 11th grade, this new lifestyle put a serious crimp in my ability to study and my grades dropped off the face of the earth. By the time I graduated, my GPA was 1.2 and I was 420 out of 430 in class rank. The only reason I graduated was because my mom pleaded with my English teacher to give me a D, so that I could finish school and go to drug rehab. Fortunately, she agreed, and three days later, I entered rehab.

Rehab was a life saver! For the first time in three years, I wasn't doing something illegal or detrimental to my body, and it was here that I was introduced to a power greater than myself. It all started one night at bedtime when a counselor was turning out our lights, and I asked him how I was supposed to turn my life and my will over to a power greater than myself. He said, "Each night, before you go to sleep, get down on your knees and place your shoes under your bed, and while there, recite the following prayer: Thank you for this day. Please help me to turn my life and my will over to you." He went on to say, "Each morning when you get up, and get down on your knees to retrieve your shoes, repeat the prayer that you recited the evening before." Discovering this power greater than myself was the first major turning point of my life, and this Higher Power could be viewed as my Inner-Genius!

Since that day more than 30 years ago, I have not once neglected to recite that prayer every night and every morning, and I have also not used drugs. My recovery continued with my thorough follow through with the remainder of the 12 steps, and six weeks later, I was released back into the loving care of my parents. I did my 90 meetings in 90 days, and this commitment to the program helped me to once again be a clean and productive member of society. However, after working minimum wage jobs for about nine months, I sensed that I might be destined for something different. Then I remembered the psychologist from high school that evaluated me and told my parents that I had low to moderate IQ and that the possibility of college was unrealistic. Fortunately, my parents had faith in my potential and offered to pay for me to attend the local community college for a semester. This was very scary, and challenging, as I really struggled for the first few months. Luckily, my mom was a reading and study skills specialist, and she taught me the crucial skills needed to get by. Eventually, I found my groove, and with the additional help of tutors, I was able to get A's and B's in most of my classes. This academic success enabled me to transfer to a four-year college, and after three more years, I walked away with a Bachelor of Science degree in Ornamental Horticulture.

With my degree in hand and my new sense of confidence, I was able to land a commissioned sales rep job in the tree care industry. It was here that I found my passion: I was a born salesman!

The second major turning point of my life occurred during a 13-week Dale Carnegie Course that I participated in back in 1995. It turns out that this was exactly what my dormant Inner-Genius was yearning for, as this course helped me to realize for the first time that conscious evolution was possible. The curriculum also ignited my interest in reading, as the course mandated that we read Carnegie's book *How to Stop Worrying and Start Living*. This was my introduction to self-improvement. Not only did it teach me that I was a worry-wart, but it also showed me how to transcend these fears with simple, practical mechanisms. The second required Carnegie book, *How to Win Friends and Influence People*, expanded on these simple life lessons. After several months of practicing these mechanisms, it became very clear that self-improvement and increased self-awareness were indeed possible. By opening my mind and heart to new ideas, my horizons were greatly expanding. My Inner-Genius was always there; it was just waiting for the right time to present itself.

It wasn't until many years later that I realized a correlation between the evolution of my consciousness and the increased presence of my Inner-Genius. The closer I moved toward the light of the virtues, the more available my Inner-Genius became, and this eventually led to the following epiphany: Unconditional lovingness, coupled with belieflessness, opens the door to unlimited creative genius.

By unlearning all preconceived notions and conditioned thoughts, I was left with a blank slate, and this open mind was the perfect environment for the intuitive guidance of the Inner-Genius to enter my conscious awareness with no resistance. And by authentically displaying unconditional love to all life in all of its expressions, I was brought back to my natural state of true worth: a condition of perfection and completeness. This state of joy and contentment welcomed the loving guidance of my Inner-Genius with an open heart.

Wow! Imagine the magnitude that this revelation could have on all of humanity. By just being kinder and more humble, we become more aware. This profound realization has dramatically impacted my life. By practicing unconditional lovingness and beliefessness, I have uncovered boundless opportunities for spiritual evolution, as intuition now floods into my conscious awareness, in the form of creativity, efficiency, inventiveness and artistry.

Book Three

Final Thoughts and Heartfelt Thanks

While sitting on the hopper, in a blissful state of belieflessness, the Universe sent me this silly pun: Arrogant know-it-alls actually know nothing, while humble know-nothings seem to know everything...

Quiet Matters

Free time is a blessing and a curse, and a strange gift from the Universe. I now understand why some monks retreat to caves for years of quiet contemplation and meditation. It is in this quietude that we see exactly how far we have evolved on our journey. In the absence of distraction, we are forced to fully be with ourselves, and in these moments, we find out precisely how content we really are. Needless to say, free time is a humbling experience.

For most of my adult life, I was a workaholic, and when I discovered that spiritual maturity was possible, I redirected all of my time and energy into voraciously seeking and striving for enlightenment. Regardless of my obsession, I have always filled my every waking moment with activities. It wasn't until fairly recently that I understood why I kept myself so busy.

My job as an arborist on a Massachusetts resort island is very seasonal. The three months of summer are extremely busy, spring and fall are moderately busy and winter is painfully slow. And it was in this dead of winter that I first discovered the wonder and the horror of free time. At first, free time felt liberating -- time to finally breathe and relax and time for reflection and quiet contemplation. However, after a short period of this wondrous reprieve, the horror of "What the hell do I do now?" barreled in like a tsunami!

It was in this vulnerable moment that my true spiritual journey began. This quietude opened the door for my Inner-Teacher to guide me through deep and honest introspection and allow me to notice and acknowledge all of the vices that were obscuring my true worth and all of the virtues that were bringing me joy. Free time gave me the opportunity to forgive myself, which led to self-compassion, self-acceptance and eventually self-love. Free time also allowed me to recognize my negative emotions as they arose and surrender them through The Letting Go Mechanism. And finally, free time enabled me to embark on the transformation process and the eventual embodiment of the virtues of peace.

Guiding Principles

Over the last 10 years I have been introduced to a variety of different paths to peace. The 10 guiding principles below summarize, in a very concise way, everything that I have uncovered. These ancient truths are the heart and Soul of this book... and of me.

1. I humbly surrender this life to Thee. I don't know anything for certain; by the grace of God, the way shall be uncovered.
2. Practice unconditional lovingness with all life in all of its expressions, starting with oneself. Begin by practicing understanding, honesty, humility, forgiveness, acceptance, patience, tolerance, gratitude, graciousness, benevolence, compassion and integrity.
3. Letting go of all negative emotions as they arise is a mechanism that naturally heals wounds.
4. Be unattached to everyone and everything, with no exceptions. Attractions and aversions no longer exist; practice devotional non-duality.
5. Realize that you are an eternal essence of the Soul, not the transitory mind and body.
6. Enlightenment is nothing more than the complete absence of resistance to what is. -Adyashanti

7. Facilitate experiential, Inner-Teacher revelations in oneself and others through appreciative inquiry whenever possible.
8. Vulnerability opens the doors to intimacy.
9. Self-forgiveness, self-acceptance and self-compassion will reveal self-love.
10. Live and Let Live.

Epilogue

Our journey began with mindfulness, which laid the groundwork for becoming the witness-observer of our emotions. Once recognized and acknowledged, we created the intention to let these emotions go through the practice of non-resistance. By virtue of self-forgiveness, self-compassion and self-acceptance, we moved closer to self-love. And by surrendering control of our lives, we invited our Inner-Teacher to guide us through the ebbs and flows of life, and this Divine essence opened our hearts and allowed the virtues of peace to gently reweave the fabric of our being.

Acknowledgment

My heartfelt gratitude goes out to the following authors and their books that helped to pave the way for this publication:

Stuart Wilde...*Infinite Self*
John Streleck...*The Why Café*
Wayne Dyer...*The Power of Intention*
Dr. David R. Hawkins...*Transcending the Levels of Consciousness*
Michael Singer...*The Untethered Soul*
Adyashanti...*Emptiness Dancing*
Eckhart Tolle...*The Power of Now*
Paulo Coehlo...*The Pilgrimage*
Terrence Real...*I Don't Want To Talk About It*
Dr. Elio Frattaroli...*Healing the Soul in the Age of the Brain*
Hermann Hesse...*Siddharta*
Mitch Albom...*Tuesdays with Morrie*
Dan Millman...*The Journeys of Socrates*
Jeffrey Archer...*Kane and Abel*
David Baldacci...*Wish You Well*
Po Bronson...*Why Do I Love These People*
Marc Pittman...*Raising Cole*
Jeannette Walls...*The Glass Castle*
Mark Rosen...*Thank You for Being Such a Pain*
John Izzo...*The Five Secrets You Must Discover Before You Die*
Dr. Edward Hallowell...*Human Moments*
Louis Lamour...*The Lonesome Gods*

Jeffrey Marx...*Season of Life*
Nicholas Sparks...*The Notebook*
William Young...*The Shack*
Susan Woods...*A Sparkle on the Water*
Hal and Sidra Stone...*Embracing Your Inner-Critic*
Shakti Gawain...*The Path of Transformation*
Neale Donald Walsch...*Conversations with God*

Sincere appreciation to Susan Goetz and Laura Devany for their proofreading expertise and editing ingenuity.

Thank you Jenna for believing in me and the virtues of peace.

Special thanks to my amusing muse and second greatest teacher, Sky Freeman. Without your loving guidance, creative energy and spiritual companionship, this book could not have been written.

And last, but certainly not least, I offer eternal gratitude to my greatest teacher, my Inner-Teacher!

Notes and References

Prelude

Hawkins, D.R., M.D., Ph.D. (Kindle edition). *Letting Go: The Pathway of Surrender.* pgs. 621, 649, 764, 774.

Book One

Zukav, G., *Loves Heals Body Mind Spirit Community.* http://holistic-alternative-practioners.com/Gary-Zukav.html.

Graham, S. & M. *Shame Resilience.* www.shameresilience.com.

The definitions for perfectionism and judgmentalism are paraphrased from www.dictionary.com.

The mirroring quote from Carl Jung is from www.brainyquote.com.

Zukav, G. & Francis, L. (Kindle edition). *The Heart of the Soul: Emotional Awareness.* p.108.

Holden, R., Ph.D. (Google electronic books). *Happiness Now!: Timeless Wisdom for Feeling Good FAST.* p. 85.

Neff, K., *The Three Elements of Self-Compassion.* http://www.self-compassion.org/what-is-self-compassion/the-three-elements-of-self-compassion.html.

Zukav, G. & Francis, L. (Kindle edition). *The Heart of the Soul: Emotional Awareness.* p.131.

The gratitude quote from Melody Beattie is from www.brainyquote.com.

Book Two

Mou, B., *The Routledge History of Chinese Philosophy. p.347.*

The courage quote from Mary Anne Radmacher is from www.goodreads.com.

The diversity definition is from Hong Tran: ASUO Multicultural Advocate. http://gladstone.uoregon.edu/~asuomca/diversityinit/definition.html.

Zukav, G. (Kindle edition). *Seat of the Soul.* p. 256.

Stutz, P., & Michels, B., *The Real Reason We Procrastinate (And What to Do About It),* http://greatist.com/happiness/how-not-to-procrastinate-reason-procrastination.

Miller, M. Ph.D. *Shame and Psychotherapy.* http://www.columbiapsych.com/shame_miller.html.

Graham, Michael C. (2014). *Facts of Life: Ten Issues of Contentment.* Outskirts Press.

The definitions of the 12 virtues are paraphrased from www.dictionary.com.

Hawkins, D.R., M.D., Ph.D. (Kindle edition). *Power vs. Force.* pgs. 203,207.

Book Three

Adyashanti. (Electronic easy read super large 24 pt. edition). *Emptiness Dancing.* p. 74.